Testimony
Before the Subcommittee on
Counterterrorism and Intelligence,
Committee on Homeland Security,
U.S. House of Representatives

For Release on Delivery
Expected at 2:00 p.m. EST
Wednesday, November 13, 2013

PERSONNEL SECURITY CLEARANCES

I0448744

Opportunities Exist to Improve Quality Throughout the Process

Statement of Brenda S. Farrell, Director
Defense Capabilities and Management

November 13, 2013

GAO Highlights

Highlights of GAO-14-186T, a testimony before the Subcommittee on Counterterrorism and Intelligence, Committee on Homeland Security, U.S. House of Representatives

PERSONNEL SECURITY CLEARANCES

Opportunities Exist to Improve Quality Throughout the Process

Why GAO Did This Study

In 2012, the DNI reported that more than 4.9 million federal government and contractor employees held or were eligible to hold a personnel security clearance. Furthermore, GAO has reported that the federal government spent over $1 billion to conduct more than 2 million background investigations in fiscal year 2011. A high quality process is essential to minimize the risks of unauthorized disclosures of classified information and to help ensure that information about individuals with criminal activity or other questionable behavior is identified and assessed as part of the process for granting or retaining clearances. Security clearances may allow personnel to gain access to classified information that, through unauthorized disclosure, can in some cases cause exceptionally grave damage to U.S. national security. Recent events, such as unauthorized disclosures of classified information, have illustrated the need for additional work to help ensure the process functions effectively and efficiently.

This testimony addresses the (1) roles and responsibilities of different executive branch agencies involved in the personnel security process; (2) different phases of the process; and (3) extent that agencies assess the quality of the process. This testimony is based on GAO work issued between 2008 and 2013 on DOD's personnel security clearance program and government-wide suitability and security clearance reform efforts. As part of that work, GAO (1) reviewed statutes, executive orders, guidance, and processes; (2) examined agency data on timeliness and quality; (3) assessed reform efforts; and (4) reviewed samples of case files for DOD personnel.

View GAO-14-186T. For more information, contact Brenda S. Farrell at (202) 512-3604 or FarrellB@gao.gov.

What GAO Found

Several agencies in the executive branch have key roles and responsibilities in the personnel security clearance process. Executive Order 13467 designates the Director of National Intelligence (DNI) as the Security Executive Agent, who is responsible for developing policies and procedures for background investigations and adjudications. The Office of Personnel Management (OPM) conducts investigations for most of the federal government. Adjudicators from agencies, such as the Departments of Defense (DOD) and Homeland Security, that request background investigations use the investigative report and consider federal adjudicative guidelines when making clearance determinations. Reform efforts to enhance the personnel security process throughout the executive branch are principally driven and overseen by the Performance Accountability Council, which is chaired by the Deputy Director for Management at the Office of Management and Budget (OMB).

Executive branch agencies rely on a multi-phased personnel security clearance process that includes requirements determination, application, investigation, adjudication, appeals (if applicable, where a clearance has been denied), and reinvestigation (for renewal or upgrade of an existing clearance). In the requirements determination phase, agency officials must determine whether positions require access to classified information. After an individual has been selected for a position that requires a personnel security clearance and the individual submits an application for a clearance, investigators—often contractors—from OPM conduct background investigations for most executive branch agencies. Adjudicators from requesting agencies use the information from these investigations and consider federal adjudicative guidelines to determine whether an applicant is eligible for a clearance. If a clearance is denied or revoked by an agency, appeals of the adjudication decision are possible. Individuals granted clearances are subject to reinvestigations at intervals that are dependent on the level of security clearance.

Executive branch agencies do not consistently assess quality throughout the security clearance process, in part because they have not fully developed and implemented metrics to measure quality in key aspects of the process. For example, GAO reported in May 2009 that, with respect to initial top secret clearances adjudicated in July 2008 for DOD, documentation was incomplete for most of OPM's investigative reports. GAO also estimated that 12 percent of the 3,500 reports did not contain the required personal subject interview. To improve the quality of investigative documentation, GAO recommended that OPM measure the frequency with which its reports met federal investigative standards. OPM did not agree or disagree with this recommendation, and as of August 2013 had not implemented it. Further, GAO reported in 2010 that agencies do not consistently and comprehensively track the reciprocity of personnel security clearances, which is an agency's acceptance of a background investigation or clearance determination completed by any authorized investigative or adjudicative agency. OPM created a metric in early 2009 to track reciprocity, but this metric does not track how often an existing security clearance was successfully honored. GAO recommended that OMB develop comprehensive metrics to track reciprocity. OMB agreed with the recommendation, but has not yet fully implemented actions to implement this recommendation.

United States Government Accountability Office

Chairman King, Ranking Member Higgins, and Members of the Subcommittee:

Thank you for the opportunity to be here to discuss the quality of the federal government's personnel security clearance process. In 2012, the Director of National Intelligence (DNI) reported that more than 4.9 million federal government and contractor employees held or were eligible to hold a security clearance,[1] posing formidable challenges to those responsible for deciding who should be granted a clearance. Personnel security clearances allow for access to classified information on a need to know basis. Federal agencies also use other processes and procedures to determine if an individual should be granted access to certain government buildings or facilities or be employed as a military, federal civilian, or contractor employee for the federal government. Separate from, but related to, personnel security clearances are determinations of suitability that the executive branch uses to ensure individuals are suitable, based on character and conduct, for federal employment in their agency or position. We have reported that the federal government spent over $1 billion to conduct more than 2 million background investigations (in support of both personnel security clearances and suitability determinations for government employment outside of the intelligence community) in fiscal year 2011.[2]

A high-quality process is essential in order to minimize the risks of unauthorized disclosures of classified information and to help ensure that information about individuals with criminal activity or other questionable behavior is identified and assessed as part of the process for granting or retaining clearances. Security clearances may allow personnel to gain access to classified information that, through unauthorized disclosure, can in some cases cause exceptionally grave damage to U.S. national security. Recent events, such as unauthorized disclosures of classified information, have illustrated both the potential consequences of such disclosures and the need for additional work on the part of federal agencies to help ensure the process functions effectively and efficiently,

---

[1] Office of the Director of National Intelligence, *2012 Report on Security Clearance Determinations* (January 2013).

[2] GAO, *Background Investigations: Office of Personnel Management Needs to Improve Transparency of Its Pricing and Seek Cost Savings*, GAO-12-197 (Washington, D.C.: Feb. 28, 2012).

so that only trustworthy individuals obtain and keep security clearances and the resulting access to classified information that clearances make possible. We have an extensive body of work on issues related to the personnel security clearance process going back over a decade. Since 2008, we have focused on the Department of Defense's (DOD) clearance program and the government-wide effort to reform the security clearance process, and have reported repeatedly on the need to build quality into the process.

My testimony today will focus on three topics related to personnel security clearances: (1) the roles and responsibilities of the different executive branch agencies involved in the personnel security clearance process, (2) the different phases of the security clearance process that are typically followed by most executive branch agencies, and (3) the extent that executive branch agencies assess the quality of the security clearance process during these different phases.

This testimony is based on our reports and testimonies issued from 2008 through 2013 on DOD's personnel security clearance program and government-wide suitability and security clearance reform efforts. A list of these related products appears at the end of my statement. As part of the work for these products, we reviewed relevant statutes and executive orders, federal guidance, and processes; examined agency personnel security clearance policies; examined agency data on the timeliness and quality of investigations and adjudications; assessed reform efforts; and reviewed a sample of investigative and adjudication files for DOD personnel. Further, as part of our ongoing effort to determine the status of agency actions to address our prior recommendations, we reviewed the current proposal to revise a relevant federal regulation regarding position designation.

The work upon which this testimony is based was conducted in accordance with generally accepted government auditing standards. Those standards require that we plan and perform the audit to obtain sufficient, appropriate evidence to provide a reasonable basis for our findings and conclusions based on our audit objectives. We believe that the evidence obtained provides a reasonable basis for our findings and conclusions based on our audit objectives. Additional details about the scope and methodology can be found in each of these related products.

Agencies' Roles and Responsibilities in the Personnel Security Clearance Process

Several agencies in the executive branch have key roles and responsibilities in the federal government's personnel security clearance process. In a 2008 memorandum, the President called for a reform of the security clearance and suitability determination processes and subsequently issued Executive Order 13467,[3] which designates the Director of National Intelligence (DNI) as the Security Executive Agent. As such, the DNI is responsible for developing policies and procedures to help ensure the effective, efficient, and timely completion of background investigations and adjudications relating to determinations of eligibility for access to classified information and eligibility to hold a sensitive position. Positions designated as sensitive are any positions within a department or agency where the occupant could bring about, by virtue of the nature of the position, a material adverse effect on national security.

Further, Executive Order 13467 established a Suitability and Security Clearance Performance Accountability Council, commonly called the Performance Accountability Council, that is accountable to the President for achieving the goals of the reform effort, which include an efficient, practical, reciprocal, and aligned system for investigating and determining eligibility for access to classified information. Under the executive order, this council is responsible for driving implementation of the reform effort, including ensuring the alignment of security and suitability processes, holding agencies accountable for implementation, and establishing goals and metrics for progress. The order also appointed the Deputy Director for Management at the Office of Management and Budget (OMB) as the chair of the council.[4] In addition, the executive order states that agency heads shall assist the Performance Accountability Council and executive agents in carrying out any function under the order, as well as implementing any policies or procedures developed pursuant to the order.

---

[3]Executive Order No. 13467, *Reforming Processes Related to Suitability for Government Employment, Fitness for Contractor Employees, and Eligibility for Access to Classified National Security Information* (June 30, 2008).

[4]The Performance Accountability Council is comprised of the Director of National Intelligence as the Security Executive Agent, the Director of OPM as the Suitability Executive Agent, and the Deputy Director for Management, Office of Management and Budget, as the chair with the authority to designate officials from additional agencies to serve as members. As of June 2012, the council included representatives from the Departments of Defense, Energy, Health and Human Services, Homeland Security, State, Treasury, and Veterans Affairs, and the Federal Bureau of Investigation.

Executive branch agencies that request background investigations use the information from investigative reports to determine whether an applicant is eligible for a personnel security clearance. Two of the agencies that grant the most security clearances are DOD and the Department of Homeland Security (DHS). DOD accounts for the majority of all personnel security clearances, and spent $787 million on suitability and security clearance background investigations in fiscal year 2011.[5] Investigators—often contractors—from Federal Investigative Services within the Office of Personnel Management (OPM)[6] conduct the investigations for most of the federal government.[7] DOD is OPM's largest customer, and its Under Secretary of Defense for Intelligence (USD(I)) is responsible for developing, coordinating, and overseeing the implementation of DOD policy, programs, and guidance for personnel, physical, industrial, information, operations, chemical/biological, and DOD Special Access Program security. Additionally, the Defense Security Service, under the authority, direction, and control of USD(I), manages and administers the DOD portion of the National Industrial Security Program[8] for the DOD components and other federal agencies by

---

[5]GAO, *Background Investigations: Office of Personnel Management Needs to Improve Transparency of Its Pricing and Seek Cost Savings,* GAO-12-197 (Washington, D.C.: Feb. 28, 2012).

[6]OPM's Federal Investigative Services employs both federal and contract investigators to conduct work required to complete background investigations. The federal staff constitutes about 25 percent of that workforce, while OPM currently also has contracts for investigative fieldwork with several investigation firms, constituting the remaining 75 percent of its investigative workforce.

[7]In 2005, the Office of Management and Budget designated OPM as the agency responsible for, among other things, the day-to-day supervision and monitoring of security clearance investigations, and for tracking the results of individual agency-performed adjudications, subject to certain exceptions. However, the Office of the Director of National Intelligence can designate other agencies as an "authorized investigative agency" pursuant to 50 U.S.C. § 3341(b)(3), as implemented through Executive Order 13467. Alternatively, under 5 U.S.C. § 1104(a)(2), OPM can redelegate any of its investigative functions subject to performance standards and a system of oversight prescribed by OPM under 5 U.S.C. § 1104(b). Agencies without delegated authority rely on OPM to conduct their background investigations while agencies with delegated authority—including the Defense Intelligence Agency, National Security Agency, National Geospatial-Intelligence Agency, Central Intelligence Agency, Federal Bureau of Investigation, National Reconnaissance Office, and Department of State—have been authorized to conduct their own background investigations.

[8]The National Industrial Security Program was established by Executive Order 12829 to safeguard Federal Government classified information that is released to contractors, licensees, and grantees of the United States Government. Executive Order 12829, *National Industrial Security Program* (Jan. 6, 1993, as amended).

agreement, as well as providing security education and training, among other things.

DHS spent more than $57 million on suitability and security clearance background investigations in fiscal year 2011. Within DHS, the Chief Security Officer develops, implements, and oversees the department's security policies, programs, and standards; delivers security training and education to DHS personnel; and provides security support to the DHS components. The Chief of DHS's Personnel Security Division, under the direction of the Chief Security Officer, has responsibility for personnel security and suitability policies, programs, and standards, including procedures for granting, denying, and revoking access to classified information as well as initiating and adjudicating personnel security and suitability background investigations and periodic reinvestigations of applicants. Within the DHS components, the component Chief Security Officers implement established personnel security directives and policies within their respective components.

The personnel security clearance process has also been the subject of congressional oversight and statutory reporting requirements. Section 3001 of the Intelligence Reform and Terrorism Prevention Act of 2004[9] prompted government-wide suitability and security clearance reform. The act required, among other matters, an annual report to Congress—in February of each year from 2006 through 2011—about progress and key measurements on the timeliness of granting security clearances. It specifically required those reports to include the periods of time required for conducting investigations and adjudicating or granting clearances. However, the Intelligence Reform and Terrorism Prevention Act requirement for the executive branch to report annually on its timeliness expired in 2011. More recently, the Intelligence Authorization Act of 2010[10] established a new requirement that the President annually report to Congress the total amount of time required to process certain security clearance determinations for the previous fiscal year for each element of the Intelligence Community.[11] The Intelligence Authorization Act of 2010

---

[9]Pub. L. No. 108-458 (2004) (relevant sections codified at 50 U.S.C. § 3341).

[10]Pub. L. No. 111-259, § 367 (2010) (codified at 50 U.S.C. § 3104).

[11]This timeliness reporting requirement applies only to the elements of the Intelligence Community; it does not cover non-intelligence agencies that were covered by the reporting requirements in the Intelligence Reform and Terrorism Prevention Act of 2004.

additionally requires that those annual reports include the total number of active security clearances throughout the United States government, to include both government employees and contractors. Unlike the Intelligence Reform and Terrorism Prevention Act of 2004 reporting requirement, the requirement to submit these annual reports does not expire.

Phases of the Personnel Security Process

To help ensure the trustworthiness and reliability of personnel in positions with access to classified information, executive branch agencies rely on a personnel security clearance process that includes multiple phases: requirements determination, application, investigation, adjudication, appeals (if applicable, where a clearance has been denied), and reinvestigation (where applicable, for renewal or upgrade of an existing clearance). Figure 1 illustrates the steps in the personnel security clearance process, which is representative of the general process followed by most executive branch agencies and includes procedures for appeals and renewals. While different departments and agencies may have slightly different personnel security clearance processes, the phases that follow are illustrative of a typical process.[12] Since 1997, federal agencies have followed a common set of personnel security investigative standards and adjudicative guidelines for determining whether federal civilian workers, military personnel, and others, such as private industry personnel contracted by the government, are eligible to hold a security clearance.

---

[12]The general process for performing a background investigation for either a secret or top secret clearance is the same; however, the level of detail and types of information gathered for a top secret clearance is more substantial than a secret clearance.

Figure 1: Phases of the Personnel Security Clearance Process

Requirements determination.
Executive branch agencies determine a position's level of sensitivity, which includes consideration of whether or not a position requires access to classified information and, if required, the level of access. This information helps inform the decision as to whether a clearance is needed. Employees in these positions must be able to obtain and maintain a security clearance to gain access to classified information.

Application.
If, during the requirements determination phase, an agency determines that a position requires a clearance, the employee completes an electronic standard form 86 application, which the requesting agency sends to the Office of Personnel Management (OPM).

Investigation.
OPM's Federal Investigative Services division—with a workforce that is 25 percent federal investigator staff and 75 percent contract investigator staff—use federal investigative standards and OPM's internal guidance to conduct the investigations.

Adjudication.
Adjudicators from the requesting agency use the information from the investigative report to determine whether to grant or deny the employee eligibility for a security clearance by considering guidelines in 13 specific areas that elicit information about (1) conduct that could raise security concerns and (2) factors that could allay those security concerns and permit granting a clearance.

Appeals.
If an adjudicator determines that the agency should deny an initial security clearance application or revoke an existing security clearance, an employee may appeal. The appeals process varies depending on a variety of factors, and may involve agency adjudicators, security appeals boards, and, in some cases, the Defense Office of Hearings and Appeals.

Periodic reinvestigation.
As long as an individual holding a personnel security clearance remains in a position requiring access to classified information, that individual is reinvestigated periodically at intervals dependent on the level of security clearance. Top secret clearance holders are reinvestigated every 5 years and secret clearance holders are reinvestigated every 10 years.

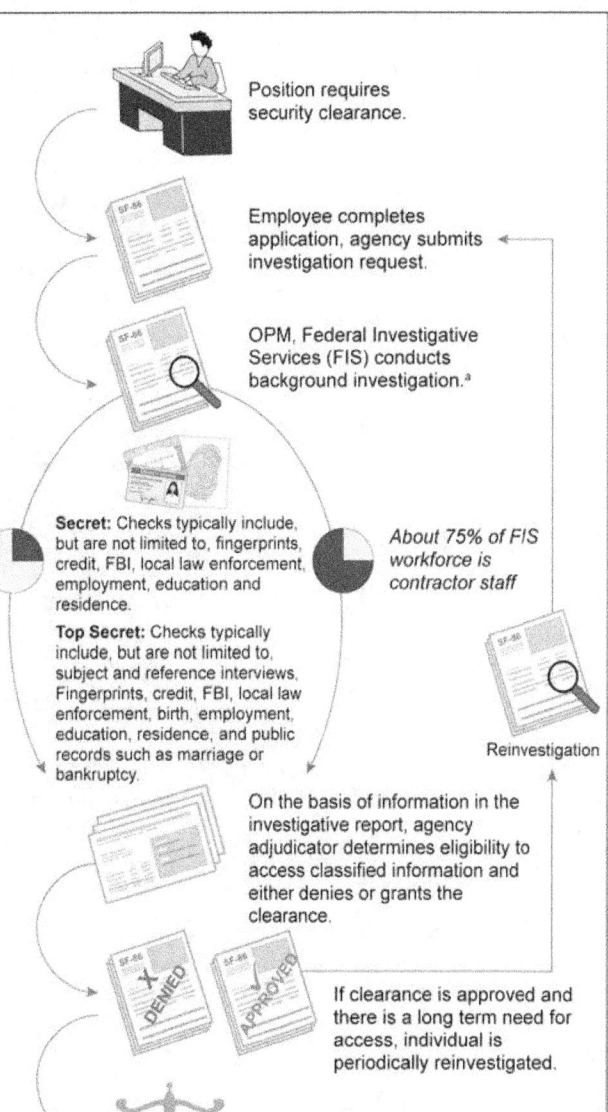

Position requires security clearance.

Employee completes application, agency submits investigation request.

OPM, Federal Investigative Services (FIS) conducts background investigation.[a]

Secret: Checks typically include, but are not limited to, fingerprints, credit, FBI, local law enforcement, employment, education and residence.

Top Secret: Checks typically include, but are not limited to, subject and reference interviews, Fingerprints, credit, FBI, local law enforcement, birth, employment, education, residence, and public records such as marriage or bankruptcy.

About 25% of FIS workforce is federal staff

About 75% of FIS workforce is contractor staff

Reinvestigation

On the basis of information in the investigative report, agency adjudicator determines eligibility to access classified information and either denies or grants the clearance.

If clearance is approved and there is a long term need for access, individual is periodically reinvestigated.

Employee may appeal if agency denies or revokes clearance.

Source: GAO analysis.

[a]OPM provides background investigation services to over 100 executive branch agencies; however, others, including some agencies in the Intelligence Community, have been delegated authority from the Office of the Director of National Intelligence, OPM, or both, to conduct their own background investigations.

Requirements Determination Phase

Executive branch agencies first determine which of their positions—military, civilian, or private-industry contractors—require access to classified information and, therefore, which people must apply for and undergo a personnel security clearance investigation. This involves assessing the risk and sensitivity level associated with that position, to determine whether it requires access to classified information and, if required, the level of access. Security clearances are generally categorized into three levels: top secret, secret, and confidential.[13] The level of classification denotes the degree of protection required for information and the amount of damage that unauthorized disclosure could reasonably be expected to cause to national defense.[14]

A sound requirements process is important because requests for clearances for positions that do not need a clearance or need a lower level of clearance increase investigative workloads and costs. A high volume of clearances continue to be processed and a sound requirements determination process is needed to effectively manage costs, since agencies spend significant amounts annually on national security and other background investigations. In addition to cost implications, limiting the access to classified information and reducing the associated risks to national security underscore the need for executive branch agencies to have a sound process to determine which positions require a security clearance.

Agency heads are responsible for designating positions within their respective agencies as sensitive if the occupant of that position could, by virtue of the nature of the position, bring about a material adverse effect

---

[13]A top secret clearance is generally also required for access to Sensitive Compartmented Information—classified intelligence information concerning or derived from intelligence sources, methods, or analytical processes that is required to be protected within formal access control systems established and overseen by the Director of National Intelligence.

[14]Unauthorized disclosure could reasonably be expected to cause (1) "damage," in the case of confidential information; (2) "serious damage," in the case of secret information; and (3) "exceptionally grave damage," in the case of top-secret information. Exec. Order No. 13526, 75 Fed. Reg. 707 (Dec. 29, 2009).

on national security.[15] In addition, Executive Order 12968, issued in 1995, makes the heads of agencies—including executive branch agencies and the military departments—responsible for establishing and maintaining an effective program to ensure that access to classified information by each employee is clearly consistent with the interests of national security. This order also states that, subject to certain exceptions, eligibility for access to classified information shall only be requested and granted on the basis of a demonstrated, foreseeable need for access. Further, part 732 of Title 5 of the Code of Federal Regulations provides requirements and procedures for the designation of national security positions, which include positions that (1) involve activities of the government that are concerned with the protection of the nation from foreign aggression or espionage, and (2) require regular use of or access to classified national security information.[16]

Part 732 of Title 5 of the Code of Federal Regulations also states that most federal government positions that could bring about, by virtue of the nature of the position, a material adverse effect on national security must be designated as a sensitive position and require a sensitivity level designation. The sensitivity level designation determines the type of background investigation required, with positions designated at a greater sensitivity level requiring a more extensive background investigation. Part 732 establishes three sensitivity levels—special-sensitive, critical-sensitive, and noncritical-sensitive—which are described in figure 2. According to OPM, positions that an agency designates as special-sensitive and critical-sensitive require a background investigation that typically results in a top secret clearance. Noncritical-sensitive positions typically require an investigation that supports a secret or confidential clearance. OPM also defines non-sensitive positions that do not have a national security element, and thus do not require a security clearance, but still require a designation of risk for suitability purposes. That risk level

---

[15]Sensitivity level is based on the potential of the occupant of a position to bring about a material adverse effect on national security. Some factors include whether the position requires access to classified information or involves the formulation of security-related policy. The sensitivity level of a position then informs the type of background investigation required of the individual in that position. The relationship between sensitivity and resulting clearances is detailed in Figure 2.

[16]Those requirements in Part 732 apply to national security positions in the competitive service, Senior Executive Service positions filled by career appointment within the executive branch, and certain excepted service positions.

informs the type of investigation required for those positions. Those investigations include aspects of an individual's character or conduct that may have an effect on the integrity or efficiency of the service.

Figure 2 illustrates the process used by both DOD and DHS to determine the need for a personnel security clearance for a federal civilian position generally used government-wide.

Figure 2: Typical Security Clearance Determination Process for Federal Civilian Positions in the Departments of Defense and Homeland Security

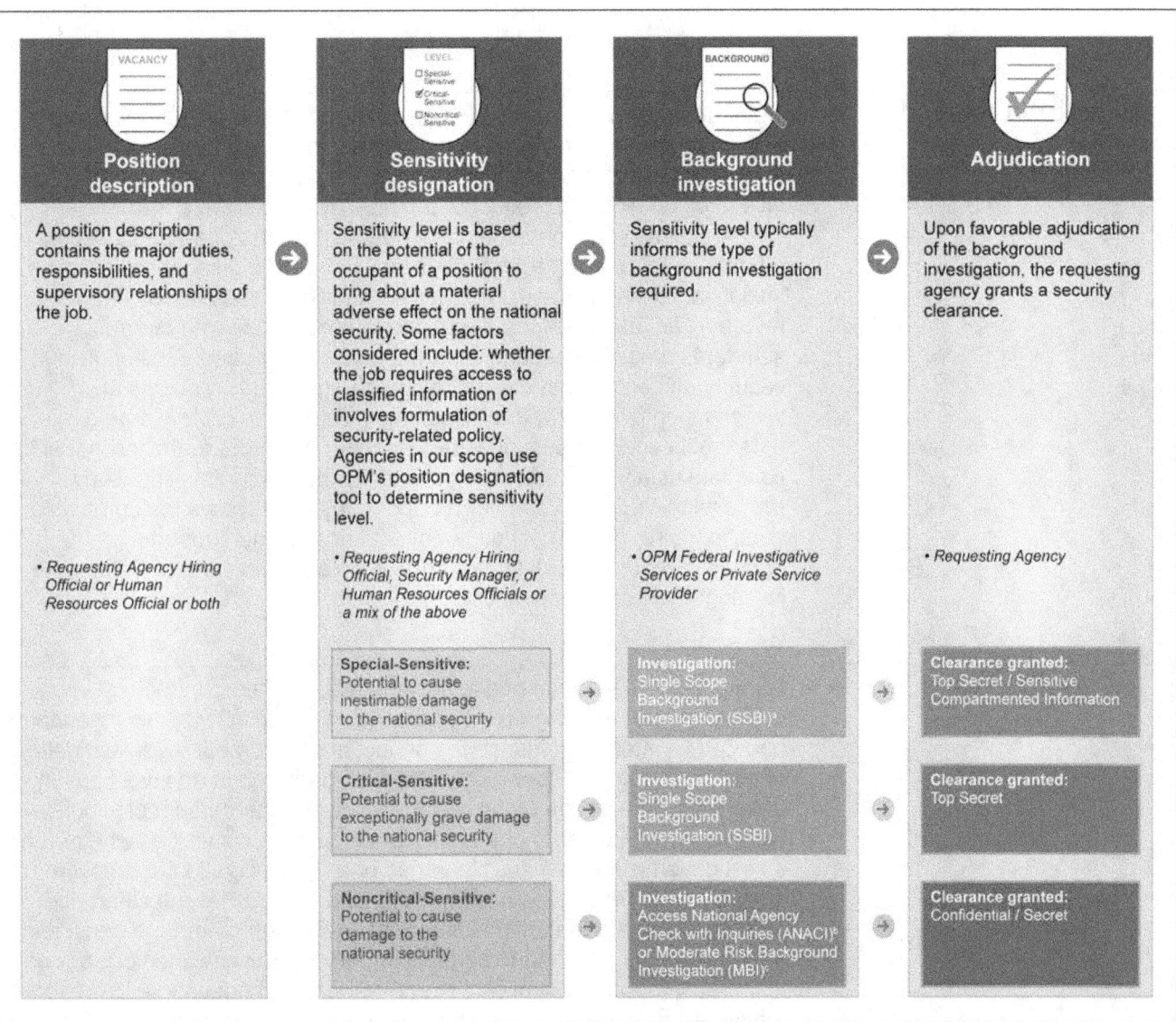

Source: GAO analysis of Department of Homeland Security (DHS) and Department of Defense (DOD) data.

[a]A Single Scope Background Investigation (SSBI) is conducted so that an individual can obtain a top secret clearance (including Sensitive Compartmented Information) and includes a review of the locations where an individual has lived, attended school, and worked. In addition, an SSBI includes interviews with four references who have social knowledge of the subject, interviews with former spouses, and a financial record check.

[b]An Access National Agency Check and Inquiries (ANACI) is used for the initial investigation for federal employees at the confidential and secret access levels. It consists of employment checks,

education checks, residence checks, reference checks, and law enforcement agency checks, as well as a National Agency Check, which includes data from military records and the Federal Bureau of Investigation's investigative index.

[c]A Moderate Risk Background Investigation (MBI) includes an ANACI and provides issue-triggered enhanced subject interviews with issue resolution. DHS uses the MBI for non-critical sensitive positions when a position is first designated as high, moderate, or low risk.

Application Phase

Once an applicant is selected for a position that requires a personnel security clearance, the applicant must obtain a security clearance in order to gain access to classified information. To determine whether an investigation would be required, the agency requesting a security clearance investigation conducts a check of existing personnel security databases to determine whether there is an existing security clearance investigation underway or whether the individual has already been favorably adjudicated for a clearance in accordance with current standards. If such a security clearance does not exist for that individual, a security officer from an executive branch agency (1) requests an investigation of an individual requiring a clearance; (2) forwards a personnel security questionnaire (Standard Form 86) to the individual to complete using OPM's electronic Questionnaires for Investigations Processing (e-QIP) system or a paper copy; (3) reviews the completed questionnaire; and (4) sends the questionnaire and supporting documentation, such as fingerprints and signed waivers, to OPM or its investigation service provider.

Investigation Phase

During the investigation phase, investigators—often contractors—from OPM's Federal Investigative Services use federal investigative standards and OPM's internal guidance to conduct and document the investigation of the applicant. The scope of information gathered in an investigation depends on the needs of the client agency and the personnel security clearance requirements of an applicant's position, as well as whether the investigation is for an initial clearance or a reinvestigation to renew a clearance. For example, in an investigation for a top secret clearance, investigators gather additional information through more time-consuming efforts, such as traveling to conduct in-person interviews to corroborate information about an applicant's employment and education. However, many background investigation types have similar components. For instance, for all investigations, information that applicants provide on electronic applications are checked against numerous databases. Both secret and top secret investigations contain credit and criminal history checks, while top secret investigations also contain citizenship, public record, and spouse checks as well as reference interviews and an Enhanced Subject Interview to gain insight into an applicant's character.

Table 1 highlights the investigative components generally associated with the secret and top secret clearance levels. After OPM, or the designated provider, completes the background investigation, the resulting investigative report is provided to the requesting agencies for their internal adjudicators.

Table 1: Information Gathered in Conducting a Typical Investigation to Determine Suitability and Eligibility for a Personnel Security Clearance

Type of information gathered by component	Type of background investigation	
	Secret	Top Secret
1. Personnel security questionnaire: The reported answers on an electronic SF-85P or SF-86 form	X	X
2. Fingerprints: Fingerprints submitted electronically or manually	X	X
3. National agency check: Data from Federal Bureau of Investigation, military records, and other agencies as required (with fingerprint)	X	X
4. Credit check: Data from credit bureaus where the subject lived/worked/attended school for at least 6 months	X	X
5. Local agency checks: Data from law enforcement agencies where the subject lived/worked/attended school during the past 10 years or—in the case of reinvestigations—since the last security clearance investigation	X	X
6. Date and place of birth: Corroboration of information supplied on the personnel security questionnaire		X
7. Citizenship: For individuals born outside of the United States, verification of U.S. citizenship directly from the appropriate registration authority		X
8. Education: Verification of most recent or significant claimed attendance, degree, or diploma	M	X
9. Employment: Review of employment records and interviews with workplace references, such as supervisors and coworkers	M	X
10. 1References: Data from interviews with subject-identified and investigator-developed leads	M	X
11. National agency check for spouse or cohabitant: Data from Federal Bureau of Investigation, military records, and other agencies as required (without fingerprint)		X
12. Former spouse: Data from interview(s) conducted with spouse(s) divorced within the last 10 years or since the last investigation or reinvestigation		X
13. Neighborhoods: Interviews with neighbors and verification of residence through records check	M	X
14. Public records: Verification of issues, such as bankruptcy, divorce, and criminal and civil court cases		X
15. Enhanced Subject Interview: Collection of relevant data, resolution of significant issues or inconsistencies	a	X

Source: DOD and OPM

Note: The content and amount of information collected as part of a personnel security clearance investigation is dependent on a variety of case-specific factors, including the history of the applicant and the nature of the position; however, items 1-15 are typically collected for the types of investigations indicated.

M = Components with this notation are checked through requests for information sent by OPM's Federal Investigative Services through the mail.

[a]The Enhanced Subject Interview was developed by the Joint Reform Team and implemented by OPM in 2011 and serves as an in-depth discussion between the interviewer and the subject to ensure

a full understanding of the applicant's information, potential issues, and mitigating factors. It is included in a Minimum Background Investigation, one type of suitability investigation, and can be triggered by the presence of issues in a secret level investigation.

In December 2012, the Office of the Director of National Intelligence (ODNI) and OPM jointly issued a revised version of the federal investigative standards for the conduct of background investigations for individuals that work for or on behalf of the federal government. According to October 31, 2013 testimony by an ODNI official, the revised standards will be implemented through a phased approach beginning in 2014 and continuing through 2017.[17]

Adjudication and Appeals Phases

During the adjudication phase, adjudicators from the hiring agency use the information from the investigative report along with federal adjudicative guidelines to determine whether an applicant is eligible for a security clearance.[18] To make clearance eligibility decisions, the adjudicative guidelines specify that adjudicators consider 13 specific areas that elicit information about (1) conduct that could raise security concerns and (2) factors that could allay those security concerns and

---

[17]Brian A. Prioletti, Assistant Director, Special Security Directorate, National Counterintelligence Executive, Office of the Director of National Intelligence, *Statement for the Record: Open Hearing on Security Clearance Reform*, testimony before the Senate Committee on Homeland Security and Governmental Affairs, 113th Cong., 1st sess., October 31, 2013.

[18]For industry personnel, the Defense Security Service (DSS) adjudicated clearance eligibility for DOD and 24 other federal agencies, by agreement, using OPM-provided investigative reports. However, DOD is in the process of consolidating its adjudication facilities, including those for industry personnel. Per DOD 5220.22-M, *National Industrial Security Program: Operating Manual* (Feb. 28, 2006 incorporating changes Mar. 28, 2013), those agencies are: (1) National Aeronautics and Space Administration; (2) Department of Commerce; (3) General Services Administration; (4) Department of State; (5) Small Business Administration; (6) National Science Foundation; (7) Department of the Treasury; (8) Department of Transportation; (9) Department of the Interior; (10) Department of Agriculture; (11) Department of Labor; (12) Environmental Protection Agency; (13) Department of Justice; (14) Federal Reserve System; (15) U.S. Government Accountability Office; (16) U.S. Trade Representative; (17) U.S. International Trade Commission; (18) U.S. Agency for International Development; (19) Nuclear Regulatory Commission; (20) Department of Education; (21) Department of Health and Human Services; (22) Department of Homeland Security; (23) Federal Communications Commission; and (24) Office of Personnel Management.

permit granting a clearance.[19] The adjudication process is a careful weighing of a number of variables, to include disqualifying and mitigating factors, known as the "whole-person" concept. For example, when a person's life history shows evidence of unreliability or untrustworthiness, questions can arise as to whether the person can be relied on and trusted to exercise the responsibility necessary for working in a secure environment where protecting national security is paramount. As part of the adjudication process, the adjudicative guidelines require agencies to determine whether a prospective individual meets the adjudicative criteria for determining eligibility, including personal conduct and financial considerations. If an individual has conditions that raise a security concern or may be disqualifying, the adjudicator evaluates whether there are other factors that mitigate such risks (such as a good-faith effort to repay a federal tax debt). On the basis of this assessment, the agency may make a risk-management decision to grant the security-clearance eligibility determination, possibly with a warning that future incidents of a similar nature may result in revocation of access.

If a clearance is denied or revoked, appeals of the adjudication decision are generally possible. We have work underway to review the process for security clearance revocations. We expect to issue a report on this process in the spring of 2014.

Reinvestigation Phase

Once an individual has obtained a personnel security clearance and as long as they remain in a position that requires access to classified national security information, that individual is reinvestigated periodically at intervals that are dependent on the level of security clearance. For example, top secret clearance holders are reinvestigated every 5 years, and secret clearance holders are reinvestigated every 10 years. Some of the information gathered during a reinvestigation would focus specifically

---

[19]Federal guidelines state that clearance decisions require a common sense determination of eligibility for access to classified information based upon careful consideration of the following 13 areas: allegiance to the United States; foreign influence; foreign preference; sexual behavior; personal conduct; financial considerations; alcohol consumption; drug involvement; emotional, mental, and personality disorders; criminal conduct; security violations; outside activities; and misuse of information technology systems. Further, the guidelines require adjudicators to evaluate the relevance of an individual's overall conduct by considering factors such as the nature, extent, and seriousness of the conduct; the circumstances surrounding the conduct, to include knowledgeable participation; the frequency and recency of the conduct; and the individual's age and maturity at the time of the conduct, among others.

on the period of time since the last approved clearance, such as a check of local law enforcement agencies where an individual lived and worked since the last investigation.

Further, the Joint Reform Team[20] began an effort to review the possibility of continuous evaluations, which would ascertain on a more frequent basis whether an eligible employee with access to classified information continues to meet the requirements for access. Specifically, the team proposed to move from periodic review to that of continuous evaluation, meaning annually for top secret and similar positions and at least once every five years for secret or similar positions, as a means to reveal security-relevant information earlier than the previous method, and provide increased scrutiny on populations that could potentially represent risk to the government because they already have access to classified information. The revised federal investigative standards state that the top secret level of security clearances may be subject to continuous evaluation.

Agencies Do Not Consistently Assess Quality Throughout the Personnel Security Clearance Process

Executive branch agencies do not consistently assess quality throughout the personnel security clearance process, in part because they have not fully developed and implemented metrics to measure quality in key aspects of the personnel security clearance process. To promote oversight and positive outcomes, such as maximizing the likelihood that individuals who are security risks will be scrutinized more closely, we have emphasized, since the late 1990s,[21] the need to build and monitor quality throughout the personnel security clearance process. While our work historically was focused on DOD, particularly since we placed DOD's personnel security clearance program on our high-risk list[22] in 2005 because of delays in completing clearances,[23] we have included

---

[20]In 2007, DOD and the Office of the Director of National Intelligence (ODNI) formed the Joint Security Clearance Process Reform Team, known as the Joint Reform Team, to improve the security clearance process government-wide.

[21]GAO, *DOD Personnel: Inadequate Personnel Security Investigations Pose National Security Risks*, GAO/NSIAD-00-12 (Washington, D.C.: Oct. 27, 1999).

[22]Every two years at the start of a new Congress, GAO issues a report that identifies government operations that are high risk due to their vulnerabilities to fraud, waste, abuse, and mismanagement, or are most in need of transformation to address economy, efficiency, or effectiveness.

[23]GAO, *High-Risk Series: An Update*, GAO-05-207 (Washington, D.C.: Jan. 1, 2005).

DHS in our most recent reviews of personnel security clearance issues. Having assessment tools and performance metrics in place is a critical initial step toward instituting a program to monitor and independently validate the effectiveness and sustainability of corrective measures.

Guidance Not Developed for Determining if Positions Require a Clearance or for Reviewing Existing Position Designations

In July 2012, we reported that the DNI, as the Security Executive Agent, had not provided agencies clearly defined policy and procedures to consistently determine if a position requires a personnel security clearance, or established guidance to require agencies to review and revise or validate existing federal civilian position designations.[24] As a result, we concluded that DHS and DOD, along with other executive branch agencies, do not have reasonable assurance that security clearance position designations are correct, which could compromise national security if positions are underdesignated, or create unnecessary and costly investigative coverage if positions are overdesignated.

In the absence of clear guidance, agencies are using a position designation tool that OPM designed to determine the sensitivity and risk levels of civilian positions that, in turn, inform the type of investigation needed.[25] This tool—namely, the Position Designation of National Security and Public Trust Positions—is intended to enable a user to evaluate a position's national security and suitability requirements so as to determine a position's sensitivity and risk levels, which in turn dictate the type of background investigation that will be required for the individual who will occupy that position. Both DOD and DHS components use the tool. In addition, DOD issued guidance in September 2011[26] and August 2012[27] requiring its personnel to use OPM's tool to determine the proper position sensitivity designation. A DHS instruction requires personnel to

---

[24]GAO, *Security Clearances: Agencies Need Clearly Defined Policy for Determining Civilian Position Requirements,* GAO-12-800 (Washington, D.C.: July 12, 2012).

[25]According to OPM's Federal Investigations Notice No. 10-06, Position Designation Requirements (Aug. 11, 2010), the tool is recommended for all agencies requesting OPM investigations and required for all positions in the competitive service, positions in the excepted service where the incumbent can be noncompetitively converted to the competitive service, and career appointments in the Senior Executive Service.

[26]DOD, Washington Headquarters Services, *Implementation of the Position Designation Automated Tool* (Sept. 27, 2011).

[27]DOD Instruction 1400.25, Volume 731, *DOD Civilian Personnel Management System: Suitability and Fitness Adjudication For Civilian Employees* (Aug. 24, 2012).

designate all DHS positions—including positions in the DHS components—by using OPM's position sensitivity designation guidance, which is the basis of the tool.[28]

OPM audits, however, have found inconsistency in these position designations, and some agencies described problems implementing OPM's tool. For example, during the course of our 2012 review, DOD and DHS officials raised concerns regarding the guidance provided through the tool and expressed that they had difficulty implementing it. Specifically, officials from DHS's U.S. Immigration and Customs Enforcement stated that the use of the tool occasionally resulted in inconsistency, such as over- or underdesignating a position, and expressed a need for additional clear, easily interpreted guidance on designating national security positions. DOD officials stated that they have had difficulty implementing the tool because it focuses more on suitability than security, and the national security aspects of DOD's positions are of more concern to them than the suitability aspects. Further, although the DNI was designated as the Security Executive Agent in 2008, ODNI officials noted that the DNI did not have input into recent revisions of OPM's position designation tool.

As a result, we recommended that the DNI, in coordination with the Director of OPM and other executive branch agencies as appropriate, issue clearly defined policy and procedures for federal agencies to follow when determining if federal civilian positions require a personnel security clearance. In written comments on our July 2012 report, the ODNI concurred with this recommendation. In May 2013, ODNI and OPM jointly drafted a proposed revision to the federal regulations on position designation which, if finalized in its current form, would provide additional requirements and examples of position duties at each sensitivity level. We also recommended that once those policies and procedures are in place, the DNI and the Director of OPM, in their roles as executive agents, collaborate to revise the position designation tool to reflect the new guidance. ODNI and OPM concurred with this recommendation and recently told us that they are in the process of revising the tool.

---

[28]DHS Management Instruction 121-01-007, *Department of Homeland Security Personnel Suitability and Security Program* (June 2009).

In July 2012, we also reported that the executive branch did not have a consistent process for reviewing and validating existing security clearance requirements for federal civilian positions.[29] According to Executive Order 12968, the number of employees that each agency determines is eligible for access to classified information shall be kept to the minimum required, and, subject to certain exceptions, eligibility shall be requested or granted only on the basis of a demonstrated, foreseeable need for access. During our 2012 review of several DOD and DHS components, we found that officials were aware of the need to keep the number of security clearances to a minimum but were not always subject to a standard requirement to review and validate the security clearance needs of existing positions on a periodic basis. We found, instead, that agencies' policies provided for a variety of practices for reviewing the clearance needs of federal civilian positions. In addition, agency officials told us that their policies were implemented inconsistently.

DOD's personnel security regulation and other guidance[30] provides DOD components with criteria to consider when determining whether a position is sensitive or requires access to classified information, and some DOD components also have developed their own guidance. According to DHS guidance, supervisors are responsible for ensuring that (1) position designations are updated when a position undergoes major changes (e.g., changes in missions and functions, job responsibilities, work assignments, legislation, or classification standards), and (2) position security designations are assigned as new positions are created. Some DHS components have additional requirements to review position designation more regularly to cover positions other than those newly created or vacant. For example, U.S. Coast Guard guidance[31] states that hiring officials and supervisors should review position descriptions even when there is no vacancy and, as appropriate, either revise or review them. In addition, according to officials in U.S. Immigration and Customs Enforcement, supervisors are supposed to review position descriptions

---

[29]GAO-12-800.

[30]DOD 5200.2-R, *Department of Defense Personnel Security Program* (January 1987, reissued incorporating changes Feb. 23, 1996), as modified by Under Secretary of Defense Memorandum, *Implementation of the Position Designation Automated Tool* (May 10, 2011).

[31]U.S. Coast Guard, CG-121, *Civilian Hiring Guide for Supervisors and Managers*, ver. 2 (June 11, 2010).

annually during the performance review process to ensure that the duties and responsibilities on the position description are up-to-date and accurate. However, officials stated that U.S. Immigration and Customs Enforcement does not have policies or requirements in place to ensure any particular level of detail in that review.

During our 2012 review, DOD and DHS officials acknowledged that overdesignating a position can result in expenses for unnecessary investigations. When a position is overdesignated, additional resources are unnecessarily spent conducting the investigation and adjudication of a background investigation that exceeds agency requirements. Without a requirement to consistently review, revise, or validate existing security clearance position designations, we concluded that executive branch agencies—such as DOD and DHS—may be hiring and budgeting for both initial and periodic security clearance investigations using position descriptions and security clearance requirements that do not reflect national security needs. Moreover, since reviews were not being done consistently, DOD, DHS, and other executive branch agencies did not have reasonable assurance that they were keeping to a minimum the number of positions that require security clearances on the basis of a demonstrated and foreseeable need for access.

Therefore, we recommended in July 2012 that the DNI, in coordination with the Director of OPM and other executive branch agencies as appropriate, issue guidance to require executive branch agencies to periodically review and revise or validate the designation of all federal civilian positions. In written comments on that report, the ODNI concurred with this recommendation and stated that as duties and responsibilities of federal positions may be subject to change, it planned to work with OPM and other executive branch agencies to ensure that position designation policies and procedures include a provision for periodic reviews. OPM stated in its written comments to our report that it would work with the DNI on guidance concerning periodic reviews of existing designations.

ODNI and OPM are currently in the process of finalizing revisions to the position designation federal regulation. As part of our ongoing processes to routinely monitor the status of agency actions to address our prior recommendations, we note that the proposed regulation would newly require agencies to conduct a one-time reassessment of position designations within 24 months of the final regulation's effective date, which is an important step towards ensuring that the current designations of national security positions are accurate. However, the national security environment and the duties and descriptions of positions may change over time, thus the importance of periodic review or validation. The proposed regulation, if finalized in its current form, would not require a periodic reassessment of positions' need for access to classified information as we recommended. We believe this needs to be done and, as part of monitoring the status of our recommendation, we will continue to review the finalized federal regulation and any related guidance that directs position designation to determine whether periodic review or validation is required.

Quality of OPM Investigative Reports Not Measured

As of August 2013, OPM had not yet implemented metrics to measure the completeness of its investigative reports—results from background investigations—although we have previously identified deficiencies in these reports. OPM supplies about 90 percent of all federal clearance investigations, including those for DOD. For example, in May 2009 we reported that, with respect to DOD initial top secret clearances adjudicated in July 2008, documentation was incomplete for most OPM investigative reports. We independently estimated that 87 percent of about 3,500 investigative reports that DOD adjudicators used to make clearance decisions were missing at least one type of documentation required by federal investigative standards.[32] The type of documentation most often missing from investigative reports was verification of all of the applicant's employment, followed by information from the required number of social references for the applicant and complete security forms. We also estimated that 12 percent of the 3,500 investigative reports did not contain a required personal subject interview. Officials within various executive branch agencies have noted to us that the information gathered during the interview and investigative portion of the process is essential for making adjudicative decisions.

At the time of our 2009 review, OPM did not measure the completeness of its investigative reports, which limited the agency's ability to explain the extent or the reasons why some reports were incomplete. As a result of the incompleteness of OPM's investigative reports on DOD personnel, we recommended in May 2009 that OPM measure the frequency with which

---

[32]Estimates in our May 2009 report were based on our review of a random sample of 100 OPM-provided investigative reports for initial top secret clearances granted in July 2008 by the U.S. Army, U.S. Navy, and U.S. Air Force central adjudication facilities and have margins of error, based on a 95 percent confidence interval, of +/- 10 percentage points or fewer.

its investigative reports meet federal investigative standards, so that the executive branch can identify the factors leading to incomplete reports and take corrective actions.[33] OPM did not agree or disagree with our recommendation.

In a subsequent February 2011 report, we noted that OMB, ODNI, DOD, and OPM leaders had provided congressional members with metrics to assess the quality of the security clearance process, including investigative reports and other aspects of the process.[34] For example, the Rapid Assessment of Incomplete Security Evaluations was one tool the executive branch agencies planned to use for measuring quality, or completeness, of OPM's background investigations.[35] However, according to an OPM official in June 2012, OPM chose not to use this tool. Instead, OPM stated that it opted to develop another tool. In following up on our 2009 recommendations, as of August 2013, OPM had not provided enough details on its tool for us to determine if the tool had met the intent of our 2009 recommendation, and included the attributes of successful performance measures identified in best practices, nor could we determine the extent to which the tool was being used.

OPM also assesses the quality of investigations based on voluntary reporting from customer agencies. Specifically, OPM tracks investigations that are (1) returned for rework from the requesting agency, (2) identified as deficient using a web-based customer satisfaction survey, or (3) identified as deficient through adjudicator calls to OPM's quality hotline. However, in our past work, we have noted that the number of investigations returned for rework is not by itself a valid indicator of the quality of investigative work because DOD adjudication officials told us that they have been reluctant to return incomplete investigations in anticipation of delays that would impact timeliness. Further, relying on agencies to voluntarily provide information on investigation quality may

---

[33]GAO, *DOD Personnel Clearances: Comprehensive Timeliness Reporting, Complete Clearance Documentation, and Quality Measures Are Needed to Further Improve the Clearance Process*, GAO-09-400 (Washington, D.C.: May 19, 2009).

[34]GAO, *High-Risk Series: An Update*, GAO-11-278 (Washington, D.C.: Feb. 2011).

[35]The Rapid Assessment of Incomplete Security Evaluations tool was developed by DOD to track the quality of investigations conducted by OPM for DOD personnel security clearance investigations, measured as a percent of investigations completed that contained deficiencies.

not reflect the quality of OPM's total investigation workload. We are beginning work to further review OPM's actions to improve the quality of investigations.

We have also reported that deficiencies in investigative reports affect the quality and timeliness of the adjudicative process. Specifically, in November 2010, we reported that agency officials who utilize OPM as their investigative service provider cited challenges related to deficient investigative reports as a factor that slows agencies' abilities to make adjudicative decisions. The quality and completeness of investigative reports directly affects adjudicator workloads, including whether additional steps are required before adjudications can be made, as well as agency costs. For example, some agency officials noted that OPM investigative reports do not include complete copies of associated police reports and criminal record checks. Several agency officials stated that in order to avoid further costs or delays that would result from working with OPM, they often choose to perform additional steps internally to obtain missing information. According to ODNI and OPM officials, OPM investigators provide a summary of police and criminal reports and assert that there is no policy requiring inclusion of copies of the original records. However, ODNI officials also stated that adjudicators may want or need entire records as critical elements may be left out of the investigator's summary. For example, according to Defense Office of Hearings and Appeals officials, in one case, an investigator's summary of a police report incorrectly identified the subject as a thief when the subject was actually the victim.

Some Steps Taken to Determine Completeness of Adjudicative Files

To address issues identified in our 2009 report regarding the quality of DOD adjudications, DOD has taken some intermittent steps to implement measures to determine the completeness of its adjudicative files. In 2009, we reported that some clearances were granted by DOD adjudicators even though some required data were missing from the OPM investigative reports used to make such determinations.[36] For example, we estimated that 22 percent of the adjudicative files for about 3,500 initial top secret clearances that were adjudicated favorably did not contain all the required documentation, even though DOD regulations

---

[36]GAO, *DOD Personnel Clearances: Comprehensive Timeliness Reporting, Complete Clearance Documentation, and Quality Measures Are Needed to Further Improve the Clearance Process*, GAO-09-400 (Washington, D.C.: May 19, 2009).

require that adjudicators maintain a record of each favorable and unfavorable adjudication decision and document the rationale for granting clearance eligibility to applicants with security concerns revealed during the investigation.[37] Documentation most frequently missing from adjudicative files was the rationale for granting security clearances to applicants with security concerns related to foreign influence, financial considerations, and criminal conduct. At the time of our 2009 review, DOD did not measure the completeness of its adjudicative files, which limited the agency's ability to explain the extent or the reasons why some files are incomplete.

In 2009, we made two recommendations to improve the quality of adjudicative files. First, we recommended that DOD measure the frequency with which adjudicative files meet requirements, so that the executive branch can identify the factors leading to incomplete files and include the results of such measurement in annual reports to Congress on clearances. In November 2009, DOD subsequently issued a memorandum that established a tool to measure the frequency with which adjudicative files meet the requirements of DOD regulation. Specifically, the DOD memorandum stated that it would use a tool called the Review of Adjudication Documentation Accuracy and Rationales, or RADAR, to gather specific information about adjudication processes at the adjudication facilities and assess the quality of adjudicative documentation. In following up on our 2009 recommendations, as of 2012, a DOD official stated that RADAR had been used in fiscal year 2010 to evaluate some adjudications, but was not used in fiscal year 2011 due to funding shortfalls. DOD stated that it restarted the use of RADAR in fiscal year 2012.

Second, we recommended that DOD issue guidance to clarify when adjudicators may use incomplete investigative reports as the basis for granting clearances. In response to our recommendation, DOD's November 2009 guidance that established RADAR also outlines the minimum documentation requirements adjudicators must adhere to when documenting personnel security clearance determinations for cases with potentially damaging information. In addition, DOD issued guidance in March 2010 that clarifies when adjudicators may use incomplete

---

[37]DOD Regulation 5200.2-R, *DOD Personnel Security Program* (Jan. 1987, incorporating changes Feb. 23, 1996).

investigative reports as the basis for granting clearances. This guidance provides standards that can be used for the sufficient explanation of incomplete investigative reports.

Extent of Clearance Reciprocity Not Measured

Executive branch agencies have not yet developed and implemented metrics to track the reciprocity of personnel security clearances, which is an agency's acceptance of a background investigation or clearance determination completed by any authorized investigative or adjudicative agency, although some efforts have been made to develop quality metrics. Executive branch agency officials have stated that reciprocity is regularly granted, as it is an opportunity to save time as well as reduce costs and investigative workloads; however, we reported in 2010 that agencies do not consistently and comprehensively track the extent to which reciprocity is granted government-wide.[38] ODNI guidance requires, except in limited circumstances, that all Intelligence Community elements "accept all in-scope[39] security clearance or access determinations." Additionally, OMB guidance[40] requires agencies to honor a clearance when (1) the prior clearance was not granted on an interim or temporary basis; (2) the prior clearance investigation is current and in-scope; (3) there is no new adverse information already in the possession of the gaining agency; and (4) there are no conditions, deviations, waivers, or unsatisfied additional requirements (such as polygraphs) if the individual is being considered for access to highly sensitive programs.

---

[38]In addition to establishing objectives for timeliness, the Intelligence Reform and Terrorism Prevention Act of 2004 established requirements for reciprocity, which is an agency's acceptance of a background investigation or clearance determination completed by any authorized investigative or adjudicative executive branch agency, subject to certain exceptions such as completing additional requirements like polygraph testing. Further, in October 2008, ODNI issued guidance on the reciprocity of personnel security clearances. ODNI, Intelligence Community Policy Guidance 704.4, *Reciprocity of Personnel Security Clearance and Access Determinations* (Oct. 2, 2008).

[39]Although there are broad federal investigative guidelines, the details and depth of an investigation varies by agency depending upon its mission.

[40]Office of Management and Budget, *Memorandum for Deputies of Executive Departments and Agencies: Reciprocal Recognition of Existing Personnel Security Clearances* (Dec. 12, 2005); Office of Management and Budget, *Memorandum for Deputies of Executive Departments and Agencies: Reciprocal Recognition of Existing Personnel Security Clearances* (July 17, 2006).

While the Performance Accountability Council has identified reciprocity as a government-wide strategic goal, we have found that agencies do not consistently and comprehensively track when reciprocity is granted, and lack a standard metric for tracking reciprocity.[41] Further, while OPM and the Performance Accountability Council have developed quality metrics for reciprocity, the metrics do not measure the extent to which reciprocity is being granted. For example, OPM created a metric in early 2009 to track reciprocity, but this metric only measures the number of investigations requested from OPM that are rejected based on the existence of a previous investigation and does not track the number of cases in which an existing security clearance was or was not successfully honored by the agency. Without comprehensive, standardized metrics to track reciprocity and consistent documentation of the findings, decision makers will not have a complete picture of the extent to which reciprocity is granted or the challenges that agencies face when attempting to honor previously granted security clearances.

In 2010, we reported that executive branch officials routinely honor other agencies' security clearances, and personnel security clearance information is shared between OPM, DOD, and, to some extent, Intelligence Community databases.[42] However, we found that some agencies find it necessary to take additional steps to address limitations with available information on prior investigations, such as insufficient information in the databases or variances in the scope of investigations, before granting reciprocity. For instance, OPM has taken steps to ensure certain clearance data necessary for reciprocity are available to adjudicators, such as holding interagency meetings to determine new data fields to include in shared data. However, we also found that the shared information available to adjudicators contains summary-level detail that may not be complete. As a result, agencies may take steps to obtain additional information, which creates challenges to immediately granting reciprocity.

Further, in 2010 we reported that because there is no government-wide standardized training and certification process for investigators and

---

[41]GAO, *Personnel Security Clearances: Progress Has Been Made to Improve Timeliness but Continued Oversight Is Needed to Sustain Momentum*, GAO-11-65 (Washington, D.C.: Nov. 19, 2010).

[42]GAO-11-65.

adjudicators, according to agency officials, a subject's prior clearance investigation and adjudication may not meet the standards of the inquiring agency. Although OPM has developed some training, security clearance investigators and adjudicators are not required to complete a certain type or number of classes. As a result, the extent to which investigators and adjudicators receive training varies by agency. Consequently, as we have previously reported, agencies are reluctant to be accountable for investigations and/or adjudications conducted by other agencies or organizations.[43] To achieve fuller reciprocity, clearance-granting agencies seek to have confidence in the quality of prior investigations and adjudications.

Consequently, we recommended in 2010 that the Deputy Director of Management, OMB, in the capacity as Chair of the Performance Accountability Council, should develop comprehensive metrics to track reciprocity and then report the findings from the expanded tracking to Congress. Although OMB agreed with our recommendation, a 2011 ODNI report found that Intelligence Community agencies experienced difficulty reporting on reciprocity. The agencies are required to report on a quarterly basis the number of security clearance determinations granted based on a prior existing clearance as well as the number not granted when a clearance existed. The numbers of reciprocal determinations made and denied are categorized by the individual's originating and receiving organizational type: (1) government to government, (2) government to contractor, (3) contractor to government, and (4) contractor to contractor. The report stated that data fields necessary to collect the information described above do not currently reside in any of the datasets available and the process was completed in an agency specific, semi-manual method. Further, the Deputy Assistant Director for Special Security of the Office of the Director of National Intelligence noted in testimony in June 2012 that measuring reciprocity is difficult, and despite an abundance of anecdotes, real data is hard to come by. To address this problem, ODNI is developing a web-based form for individuals to submit their experience with reciprocity issues to the ODNI. According to ODNI, this will allow them to collect empirical data, perform systemic trend analysis, and assist agencies with achieving workable solutions.

---

[43]GAO, *Personnel Clearances: Key Factors to Consider in Efforts to Reform Security Clearance Processes*, GAO-08-352T (Washington, D.C.: Feb. 27, 2008).

Recent Efforts and Sustained Leadership Could Facilitate Progress in Assessing Quality

Several efforts are underway to review the security clearance process, and those efforts, combined with sustained leadership attention, could help facilitate progress in assessing and improving the quality of the security clearance process. After the September 16, 2013 shooting at the Washington Navy Yard, the President directed the Office of Management and Budget, in coordination with ODNI and OPM, to conduct a government-wide review into the oversight, nature, and implementation of security and suitability standards for federal employees and contractors. In addition, in September 2013, the Secretary of Defense directed an independent review to identify and recommend actions that address gaps or deficiencies in DOD programs, policies, and procedures regarding security at DOD installations and the granting and renewal of security clearances for DOD employees and contractor personnel. The primary objective of this review is to determine whether there are weaknesses in DOD programs, policies, or procedures regarding physical security at DOD installations and the security clearance and reinvestigation process that can be strengthened to prevent a similar tragedy.

As previously discussed, DOD and DHS account for the majority of security clearances within the federal government. We initially placed DOD's personnel security clearance program on our high-risk list in 2005 because of delays in completing clearances.[44] It remained on our list until 2011 because of ongoing concerns about delays in processing clearances and problems with the quality of investigations and adjudications. In February 2011, we removed DOD's personnel security clearance program from our high-risk list largely because of the department's demonstrated progress in expediting the amount of time processing clearances.[45] We also noted DOD's efforts to develop and implement tools to evaluate the quality of investigations and adjudications.

Even with the significant progress leading to removal of DOD's program from our high-risk list, the Comptroller General noted in June 2012 that sustained leadership would be necessary to continue to implement,

---

[44]GAO, *High-Risk Series: An Update*, GAO-05-207 (Washington, D.C.: Jan. 1, 2005).

[45]GAO, *High-Risk Series: An Update*, GAO-11-278 (Washington, D.C.: Feb. 2011).

monitor, and update outcome-focused performance measures.[46] The initial development of some tools and metrics to monitor and track quality not only for DOD but government-wide were positive steps; however, full implementation of these tools and measures government-wide have not yet been realized. While progress in DOD's personnel security clearance program resulted in the removal of this area from our high-risk list, significant government-wide challenges remain in ensuring that personnel security clearance investigations and adjudications are high-quality. However, if the oversight and leadership that helped address the timeliness issues focuses now on the current problems associated with quality, we believe that progress in helping executive branch agencies to assess the quality of the security clearance process could be made.

In conclusion, to avoid the risk of damaging, unauthorized disclosures of classified information, oversight of the reform efforts to measure and improve the quality of the security clearance process are imperative next steps. The progress that was made with respect to expediting the amount of time processing clearances would not have been possible without committed and sustained congressional oversight and the leadership of the Performance Accountability Council. Further actions are needed now to fully develop and implement metrics to oversee quality at every step in the process. We will continue to monitor the outcome of the agency actions discussed above to address our outstanding recommendations.

Chairman King, Ranking Member Higgins, and Members of the Subcommittee, this concludes my prepared statement. I would be pleased to answer any questions that you or other Members of the Subcommittee may have at this time.

GAO Contacts and Acknowledgment

For further information on this testimony, please contact Brenda S. Farrell, Director, Defense Capabilities and Management, who may be reached at (202) 512-3604 or farrellb@gao.gov. Contact points for our Offices of Congressional Relations and Public Affairs may be found on the last page of this statement. GAO staff who made key contributions to this testimony include David E. Moser (Assistant Director), Jim Ashley, Renee S. Brown, Ryan D'Amore, and Michael Willems.

---

[46]GAO, *Personnel Security Clearances: Continuing Leadership and Attention Can Enhance Momentum Gained from Reform Effort*, GAO-12-815T (Washington, D.C.: June 21, 2012).

Related GAO Products

Personnel Security Clearances: Full Development and Implementation of Metrics Needed to Measure Quality of Process. GAO-14-157T. Washington, D.C.: October 31, 2013.

Personnel Security Clearances: Further Actions Needed to Improve the Process and Realize Efficiencies. GAO-13-728T. Washington, D.C.: June 20, 2013.

Managing for Results: Agencies Should More Fully Develop Priority Goals under the GPRA Modernization Act. GAO-13-174. Washington, D.C.: April 19, 2013.

Security Clearances: Agencies Need Clearly Defined Policy for Determining Civilian Position Requirements. GAO-12-800. Washington, D.C.: July 12, 2012.

Personnel Security Clearances: Continuing Leadership and Attention Can Enhance Momentum Gained from Reform Effort. GAO-12-815T. Washington, D.C.: June 21, 2012.

2012 Annual Report: Opportunities to Reduce Duplication, Overlap and Fragmentation, Achieve Savings, and Enhance Revenue. GAO-12-342SP. Washington, D.C.: February 28, 2012.

Background Investigations: Office of Personnel Management Needs to Improve Transparency of Its Pricing and Seek Cost Savings. GAO-12-197. Washington, D.C.: February 28, 2012.

GAO's 2011 High-Risk Series: An Update. GAO-11-394T. Washington, D.C.: February 17, 2011.

High-Risk Series: An Update. GAO-11-278. Washington, D.C.: February 16, 2011.

Personnel Security Clearances: Overall Progress Has Been Made to Reform the Governmentwide Security Clearance Process. GAO-11-232T. Washington, D.C.: December 1, 2010.

Personnel Security Clearances: Progress Has Been Made to Improve Timeliness but Continued Oversight Is Needed to Sustain Momentum. GAO-11-65. Washington, D.C.: November 19, 2010.

DOD Personnel Clearances: Preliminary Observations on DOD's Progress on Addressing Timeliness and Quality Issues. GAO-11-185T. Washington, D.C.: November 16, 2010.

Personnel Security Clearances: An Outcome-Focused Strategy and Comprehensive Reporting of Timeliness and Quality Would Provide Greater Visibility over the Clearance Process. GAO-10-117T. Washington, D.C.: October 1, 2009.

Personnel Security Clearances: Progress Has Been Made to Reduce Delays but Further Actions Are Needed to Enhance Quality and Sustain Reform Efforts. GAO-09-684T. Washington, D.C.: September 15, 2009.

Personnel Security Clearances: An Outcome-Focused Strategy Is Needed to Guide Implementation of the Reformed Clearance Process. GAO-09-488. Washington, D.C.: May 19, 2009.

DOD Personnel Clearances: Comprehensive Timeliness Reporting, Complete Clearance Documentation, and Quality Measures Are Needed to Further Improve the Clearance Process. GAO-09-400. Washington, D.C.: May 19, 2009.

High-Risk Series: An Update. GAO-09-271. Washington, D.C.: January 2009.

Personnel Security Clearances: Preliminary Observations on Joint Reform Efforts to Improve the Governmentwide Clearance Eligibility Process. GAO-08-1050T. Washington, D.C.: July 30, 2008.

Personnel Clearances: Key Factors for Reforming the Security Clearance Process. GAO-08-776T. Washington, D.C.: May 22, 2008.

Employee Security: Implementation of Identification Cards and DOD's Personnel Security Clearance Program Need Improvement. GAO-08-551T. Washington, D.C.: April 9, 2008.

Personnel Clearances: Key Factors to Consider in Efforts to Reform Security Clearance Processes. GAO-08-352T. Washington, D.C.: February 27, 2008.

DOD Personnel Clearances: DOD Faces Multiple Challenges in Its Efforts to Improve Clearance Processes for Industry Personnel. GAO-08-470T. Washington, D.C.: February 13, 2008.

DOD Personnel Clearances: Improved Annual Reporting Would Enable More Informed Congressional Oversight. GAO-08-350. Washington, D.C.: February 13, 2008.

DOD Personnel Clearances: Delays and Inadequate Documentation Found for Industry Personnel. GAO-07-842T. Washington, D.C.: May 17, 2007.

High-Risk Series: An Update. GAO-07-310. Washington, D.C.: January 2007.

DOD Personnel Clearances: Additional OMB Actions Are Needed to Improve the Security Clearance Process. GAO-06-1070. Washington, D.C.: September 28, 2006.

DOD Personnel Clearances: New Concerns Slow Processing of Clearances for Industry Personnel. GAO-06-748T. Washington, D.C.: May 17, 2006.

DOD Personnel Clearances: Funding Challenges and Other Impediments Slow Clearances for Industry Personnel. GAO-06-747T. Washington, D.C.: May 17, 2006.

DOD Personnel Clearances: Government Plan Addresses Some Long-standing Problems with DOD's Program, But Concerns Remain. GAO-06-233T. Washington, D.C.: November 9, 2005.

DOD Personnel Clearances: Some Progress Has Been Made but Hurdles Remain to Overcome the Challenges That Led to GAO's High-Risk Designation. GAO-05-842T. Washington, D.C.: June 28, 2005.

High-Risk Series: An Update. GAO-05-207. Washington, D.C.: January 2005.

DOD Personnel Clearances: Preliminary Observations Related to Backlogs and Delays in Determining Security Clearance Eligibility for Industry Personnel. GAO-04-202T. Washington, D.C.: May 6, 2004.

GAO's Mission	The Government Accountability Office, the audit, evaluation, and investigative arm of Congress, exists to support Congress in meeting its constitutional responsibilities and to help improve the performance and accountability of the federal government for the American people. GAO examines the use of public funds; evaluates federal programs and policies; and provides analyses, recommendations, and other assistance to help Congress make informed oversight, policy, and funding decisions. GAO's commitment to good government is reflected in its core values of accountability, integrity, and reliability.
Obtaining Copies of GAO Reports and Testimony	The fastest and easiest way to obtain copies of GAO documents at no cost is through GAO's website (http://www.gao.gov). Each weekday afternoon, GAO posts on its website newly released reports, testimony, and correspondence. To have GAO e-mail you a list of newly posted products, go to http://www.gao.gov and select "E-mail Updates."
Order by Phone	The price of each GAO publication reflects GAO's actual cost of production and distribution and depends on the number of pages in the publication and whether the publication is printed in color or black and white. Pricing and ordering information is posted on GAO's website, http://www.gao.gov/ordering.htm. Place orders by calling (202) 512-6000, toll free (866) 801-7077, or TDD (202) 512-2537. Orders may be paid for using American Express, Discover Card, MasterCard, Visa, check, or money order. Call for additional information.
Connect with GAO	Connect with GAO on Facebook, Flickr, Twitter, and YouTube. Subscribe to our RSS Feeds or E-mail Updates. Listen to our Podcasts. Visit GAO on the web at www.gao.gov.
To Report Fraud, Waste, and Abuse in Federal Programs	Contact: Website: http://www.gao.gov/fraudnet/fraudnet.htm E-mail: fraudnet@gao.gov Automated answering system: (800) 424-5454 or (202) 512-7470
Congressional Relations	Katherine Siggerud, Managing Director, siggerudk@gao.gov, (202) 512-4400, U.S. Government Accountability Office, 441 G Street NW, Room 7125, Washington, DC 20548
Public Affairs	Chuck Young, Managing Director, youngc1@gao.gov, (202) 512-4800 U.S. Government Accountability Office, 441 G Street NW, Room 7149 Washington, DC 20548

Please Print on Recycled Paper.

www.ingramcontent.com/pod-product-compliance
Lightning Source LLC
Chambersburg PA
CBHW080734290526
45790CB00008B/3186